D0438689

Written by Justine Fontes
Illustrated by Charles Jordan

Children's Press®
A Division of Scholastic Inc.
New York • Toronto • London • Auckland • Sydney
Mexico City • New Delhi • Hong Kong
Danbury, Connecticut

To Timmy and all the other kids at Dukenfields Toy Store
—J.F.

For polite children everywhere
—C.J.

Reading Consultants

Linda Cornwell
Literacy Specialist

Katharine A. Kane
Education Consultant
(Retired, San Diego County Office of Education and San Diego State University)

Library of Congress Cataloging-in-Publication Data

Fontes, Justine.
Rude Ralph / written by Justine Fontes ; illustrated by Charles Jordan.
p. cm. – (Rookie reader)
Summary: Rude Ralph only learns to be polite after no one will play with him.
ISBN 0-516-24567-8 (lib. bdg.) 0-516-26820-1 (pbk.)
[1. Behavior–Fiction. 2. Etiquette–Fiction.] I. Jordan, Charles, ill. II. Title. III. Series.
PZ7.F73576Ru 2003
[E]–dc21

2003007123

1 2 3 4 5 6 7 8 9 10 R 13 12 11 10 09 08 07 06 05 04

My friend Ralph is rude.

Ralph always cuts in line.

He never says, "I'm sorry."

He never says, “Excuse me.”

Ralph never shares.

Ralph never says, “May I please?”

Tristan bumps into me.
He says "Excuse me."

Tristan lets me finish what I am saying. He waits his turn to talk.

Tristan asks, "May I please?"
before he takes something of mine.

Tristan shares.

Tristan says, "Thank you."

Sometimes Tristan lets me go first.

Ralph wants to play with us.
I tell Ralph I would rather play
with someone who is polite.

Ralph says, "I can be polite."
I say, "Okay."

Ralph isn't rude anymore.
He says he'd rather have friends.

Word List (63 words)

always
am
anymore
asks
be
before
bumps
can
cuts
excuse
finish
first
friend
friends
go
have
he
he'd
his
I
I'm
in
into
is
isn't
lets
line
may
me
mine
my
never
of
okay
play
please
polite
Ralph
rather
rude
say
saying
says
shares
someone
something
sometimes
sorry
takes
talk
tell
thank
to
Tristan
turn
us
waits
wants
what
who
with
would
you

About the Author

Justine Fontes and her husband, Ron, hope to write 1001 children's books. So far they have written board books, biographies, and everything in between!

About the Illustrator

Charles Jordan lives in Pennsylvania with his wife and two children, Charlie and Maggie.